Christmas Events and Moments

Captured via

HAIKU POETRY

Burt L. Lemen

THE EMPIRE
PUBLISHERS

12808 West Airport Blvd Suite 270M Sugar Land, TX 77478,
Unites States

https://www.theempirepublishers.com/

Our books may be purchased in bulk for promotional, educational, or business use.

Please contact The Empire Publishers at +1 844 636-4579, or by email at support@theempirepublishers.com

First Edition December 2025

Foreword

Haiku has a Japanese origin with three sentences of 5-7-5 syllables in line order. This book represents a third offering of the types of haiku poetry I have written over the years, and I have been encouraged to continue to write haiku poetry. My first two books, Sharing Moments of Life and Love crafted over a Lifetime and shared via Haiku Poetry and Annual Events and Moments captured via Haiku Poetry, were well received. (On a personal note, I have also been asked over the years to write Haiku poems for friends and family for wedding services and for funerals. It seems some of my work has hit some folks in the heart. My hope is that some of these poems can do that for you. Plus, on top of that, I am a Christmas Nut, which makes writing this book a special holiday moment for me.)

Dedication:

To my Mom and Dad, Mildred and William Lemen Sr., along with my sons, Michael, Matthew, and Mark, and my brother and sister, William Lemen Jr. and Sue Lemen-Paul. Plus, I want to acknowledge a very special, loving, and sweet supportive lady in my life, Denise Moore. You all have all given me inspiration from time to time for the various Haiku topics I have written about over the years.

Dedication Haiku:

Thank you to you all,
What a nice journey I'm on,
Wishing you the best.

Burt L Lemen

Table of Contents

1.0) Christmas Beginnings

1.1

Joseph and Mary,
Traveled far for their baby,
For a free birthplace.

1.2

A baby was born,
In a stall in Bethlehem,
Holy Son of God.

1.3

It's Jesus' birthday,
Merry Christmas to you all.
Take time to give thanks.

1.4

Pause to remember,
What makes this season special?
It's more than just gifts.

1.5

Jesus, the reason,
For this Holiday Season,
He's the son of God.

1.6

Winter Holidays,
Really start with Thanksgiving,
Enjoy these moments.

2.0) Christmas Tree Memories

2.1

We get to go out,
To cut down a Christmas Tree,
What a special task.

2.2

The fresh smell of pine,
Setting up the Christmas Tree,
Make sure it's set straight.

2.3

Keep the tree watered,
Helps to keep tree fresh longer,
Sad, but needles fall.

2.4

We got a new tree,
It's an artificial one,
Needle headaches gone.

2.5

Artificial trees,
Can be put up earlier,
To enjoy longer.

2.6

Our cat loved our tree,
Ornament playtime heaven,
Glass ones were his fav's.

2.7

Work to keep your pets,
Away from your Christmas Tree,
Great stress reducer.

2.8

Pickle ornament,
Left by Santa on the tree,
Find it for a gift.

2.9

My, how a pine tree,
Stands out when others lose leaves,
Evergreens enjoyed.

3.0) Decorating the House

3.1

Bring out the holly,
Greenery makes Christmas special,
Holiday accents.

3.2

Hang that Christmas wreath,
In a spot all can enjoy,
Hang it with a bow.

3.3

Strings of lights bring smiles.
Making holiday memories,
Enjoy these moments.

3.4

I have a neighbor,
Decorates like Clark Griswold,
Lots of cars at night.

3.5

Gingerbread Houses,
Are fun to make and display,
Plus, not bad to eat.

3.6

Nativity scenes,
Serve as a nice reminder,
How Christmas began.

3.7

Hang the mistletoe,
Make sure you and your sweetie,
Pause to get a kiss.

3.8

Advent Calendars.
Used to count down Christmas days,
With candies and treats.

3.9

I have a special,
Over a 100 years old.
Advent Calendar.

4.0) Special Meals and Treats

4.1

The Christmas cookies,
A Holiday tradition,
Fun to make and eat.

4.2

Make sure Santa gets,
A glass of milk and cookies,
Keep "Santa" happy.

4.3

Cooked Turkey and Ham,
Make Christmas dinner special,
Plus, days after meals.

4.4

Turkey with gravy,
A special combination,
What a nice taste treat.

4.5

Enjoy Christmas meals,
They're special times with family,
And for your close friends.

4.6

Special meals enjoyed,
With special friends and family,
Holiday cooking.

4.7

A glass of eggnog,
Served with those Christmas cookies,
What a nice dessert. (-Or- What a nice breakfast.)

4.8

Make Christmas candy,
With chocolate, fruit, and some nuts,
Share with your family.

4.9

Enjoy candy canes.
Good to eat or hang on tree,
Peppermint's the best.

4.10

It is amazing,
The stories told of loved ones,
At holiday meals.

5.0) Christmas Parties

5.1

A special sweater,
For ugly sweater parties,
Go on, have some fun.

5.2

Have some office fun,
Plan that holiday party,
Make your staff happy.

5.3

White elephant gifts,
Can be a party highlight,
A different memory.

5.4

Secret Santas can,
Make some holiday fun time.
Who got me this gift?

5.5

Holiday parties,
To be enjoyed with much fun,
Breaks from the routine.

5.6

My kids smiled with glee,
When Santa came to party,
Handing out candy.

5.7

I still remember,
My Mom's last Christmas party,
She passed within months.

6.0) Special Christmas Movies and Shows

6.1

A Wonderful Life,
Enjoyed over many years,
A family favorite,

6.2

Ebenezer Scrooge,
With ghosts to highlight season,
And Tiny Tim too.

6.3

Charlie Brown's special,
Highlighted the real reason,
For Christmas season.

6.4

It's a White Christmas,
A nice holiday movie,
Bing Crosby highlight.

6.5

Twelve days of Christmas,
A nice song for the season,
A song of true love.

6.6

The Grinch had his show,
That told of his shortcomings,
My kids were Grinch scared.

7.0) Christmas Songs

7.1

Sing about Rudolf,
His red nose made him famous,
Burl Ives sang his tune.

7.2

Twelve days of Christmas,
Is a nice holiday song,
A song of true love.

7.3

Grandma got run down,
By Old Santa Claus one night,
Watch for reindeer sleighs.

7.4

What a special time,
To wish you Merry Christmas,
And happy New Year.

7.5

Even Mister Grinch,
Got a holiday moment,
With a special song.

8.0) December Cold Weather Activities

8.1

Let's make that snowman,
Get that special hat and scarf,
Some snow family fun.

8.2

Sledding down that hill,
Special time with kids was shared,
Being a kid again.

8.3

Throwing some snowballs,
Can provide some smiles and laughs,
Watch out, incoming.

8.4

A snow fort was made,
With some large rolled-up snowballs,
Many days enjoyed.

8.5

I remember when,
My kids made some snow angels,
A photo moment.

8.6

What special moments,
Watching as our Basset Hound,
Frolicked in the snow.

8.7

It's snow time again,
Winter weather's here with us,
Time for coats and boots.

8.8

There's snow on the ground.
How peaceful the scenery looks,
All quiet and white.

8.9

Time to shovel snow,
Snow challenges of winter,
Clean streets, safe travel.

8.10

Holiday parades,
Can be nice family events,
When kids are happy.

8.11

Santa makes the scene,
Usually in Christmas parades,
Be good, he's watching.

9.0) Santa Claus Memories

9.1

With St. Nicholas
The Santa Claus traditions,
Took root and has grown.

9.2

Santa comes this month,
Were you a good boy or girl?
He knows if you're good.

9.3

Time to write Santa,
That special year-end letter,
Don't be too greedy.

9.4

We went to the mall,
To make a Santa visit,
Pictures were taken.

9.5

My little one was,
Scared first time seeing Santa,
Some nervous tears shed.

9.6

My dad played Santa,
At work holiday parties,
A lasting memory.

9.7

My nephew loved Elf,
A movie with Santa Claus,
He liked that Santa.

10.0) Christmas Friend and Family Time

10.1

We'd help my Great Aunt,
Decorate her apartment,
For Christmas Season.

10.2

Christmas break from school,
Provided holiday fun,
At home with family.

10.3

As we got older,
We got to go caroling,
With neighbors and friends.

10.4

Take time to visit,
Nursing home family members,
Well worth the time spent.

10.5

Christmas morning time,
Opening those special gifts,
Santa left for us.

10.6

Happy Holidays,
Take time for those we hold dear,
Time is a great gift.

10.7

Wishing a Merry,
Christmas to you and family,
Happy Holidays.

10.8

My aunts and uncles.
Would travel in December,
To warm Florida.

10.9

Special family time,
In warm Florida was nice.
Christmas breaks from school/work.

11.0) Christmas Crafts and Art

11.1

My kids love Christmas,
We made special ornaments,
To hang on our tree.

11.2

Some of this artwork,
Has survived the test of time,
Now hung in their trees.

11.3

Christmas cards got made,
My Aunt was the glitter queen,
These cards were special.

11.4

Construction paper,
When cut and taped in loops,
Makes some nice garland.

11.5

We would paint pine cones,
With gold spray paint and glitter,
Hung with red ribbon.

11.6

I paint in spoon bowls,
Capturing scenes of Christmas,
Snowmen turn out cute.

11.7

My Christmas artwork,
Has been sold in local shops,
Makes Christmas special.

11.8

Make snowflake doilies,
Use some starch to firm up flakes,
A holiday treat.

11.9

Cards with kids' hand prints,
Serve as a moment in time,
Kids sure grow up fast.

12.0) Make Time to Reflect on this Past Year

12.1

Take time to give thanks,
We live in a special place,
It's land of the free.

12.2

Many blessings shared,
Well beyond Christmas Season.
Take time to see them.

12.3

I always reflect,
On highlights from previous year,
And some low ones too.

12.4

Choose to stay the course,
On your positives in life,
Build on these moments.

12.5

Wishing a Merry,
Christmas to you and family,
Happy Holidays.

13.0 Christmas Cards

13.1

I have a box full,
With heartfelt past Christmas Cards,
Very nice memories.

13.2

Make time to send cards,
During Christmas Holidays,
Family remembered.

13.3

My aunt sent letters,
To loved ones at Christmas time,
Her annual recap.

13.4

Some cards contained pics.
Capturing family moments,
Kids sure grow up fast.

13.5

My Uncle loved dogs,
The doggie pictures were cute,
Dressed up as Santa. (-OR- Dressed up as an elf.)

13.6

Some cards play music,
With some animation fun,
Elves that sing and dance.

14.0) A New Year is Coming

14.1

Make resolutions,
To be the best you can be.
For now and new year.

14.2

Watching the "ball" drop,
A new year gets ushered in.
From Times Square, New York.

14.3

End of year parties,
Out with old and in with new,
Strive to be better.

14.4

Challenge your young ones,
To become the best they can,
All throughout the year.

14.5

I have a wish list,
Health for our friends and family,
For this coming year.

Back Page –

Christmas Events and Memories Captured via Haiku Poetry

I want to thank you for taking the time to buy and read the poems in this book. After the release of my first two books, I had several friends and family members asking me if another book was in the works. It seems I am always writing some haiku poems for some special occasion, and Christmas is a special occasion. Being a Christmas "Elf" this book almost wrote itself. I want to wish you nothing but the best, and I hope that if any of these haiku poems resonate with you or serve as "food for positive thought", please take the time to "pay it forward" with family and friends. Time spent with loved ones is a very special gift.

Parting Haikus

Thanks for your support,
I don't take things for granted.
Each day is a gift.

I hope this book will,
Make a holiday ripple,
In your pond of life.

Happy Holidays,
Wishing you Merry Christmas,
And Happy New Year.

www.ingramcontent.com/pod-product-compliance
Lightning Source LLC
Chambersburg PA
CBHW061723120626
46550CB00003B/1333